Spy Skills
for
Girls

By
Devon Danby

Bright Green Books

Published by Bright Green Books
www.brightgreenbooks.com

First Print Edition: December 2014

First Electronic Edition: December 2011

ISBN: 978-0-9878766-2-1

How to be a Spygirl

A message from Devon

Sooner or later, every girl needs to do a little spying.

Why is your best friend acting strangely?

What does that sneaky boy keep hiding in his backpack?

To find out, you need skills. Spy skills.

And I'm just the girl to teach you.

I'm Devon Danby and I'm a spy. Well, actually, I'm not REALLY Devon Danby. That's a fake name.

But the spy part is true.

My spy training started back in grade three. I had to go to special classes every day after school and on weekends. Imagine all the fun times I missed out on!

Luckily, you don't have to worry about any of that. I've packed all my best spy skills into this one little book.

Once you've learned these basic skills, be sure to share them with your best Spygirl friends!

Now, on to your training...

Devon

Why spy?

The truth is, most people spy everyday.

Do you notice where your dad hides his favourite cookies? Do you know what time your mom takes her shower? Do you know which way your friend walks home from school? That's like spying. Only spying is much more than that.

When you spy, you make a plan to find out information. Who to watch. When to watch. What's important and what's not.

Sometimes, you can spy on your own. But most of the time, it's easier to have another Spygirl help you out. And more fun, too!

Powers of observation

Every good spy needs to keep their eyes open and remember what they see. Even a small detail can turn out to be very important.

Take notice of what people wear, how they walk and who they talk to. Watch to see if they are passing objects or messages to anyone.

Most people follow patterns of movement. Where does the suspect go and at what time? When do they eat dinner? Keep notes and soon you'll know where to find your suspect without having to follow them around all day.

Spy tip: Want to confuse an enemy spy? Change your patterns. If you usually walk the dog before you eat breakfast, try doing it the other way around once in a while.

Spy words

Let's start by going over some important spy words.

Spy
A spy uncovers information about suspicious people and what they are doing.

Spygirl
You are a Spygirl! Ask your best friends if they want to be Spygirls, too!

Spy Kit
An easy-to-carry container that contains small but important spy gear.

Spy Bag
A larger bag to hold your Spy Kit and other supplies, like disguises.

Suspect

Any suspicious person could be your suspect.

Decoy

A decoy is a fake message. It could be left by a suspect to confuse you. Or, you could use a decoy to confuse your suspect!

Drop

When you leave a message or an object for another Spygirl, the place you leave it is called a drop.

Shadowing

Following your suspect without them noticing is called shadowing.

Tail

A tail is someone who shadows another person.

Shadowing

Following your suspect can be tricky. If you act strangely, they will become suspicious. Here are some tricks to blending in.

Use your eyes

Watch your suspect with your eyes, not with your whole body. Don't move your head or shoulders. Just shift your eyes from side to side. This is easier with sunglasses on.

Stops and starts

Don't copy your suspect's moves. If they stop, keep moving until you have a good reason to stop. If they start moving, wait before you follow. Keep your distance.

Check your mirror

Pretend you're not watching at all. Turn your back on your suspect. Pull out a small mirror and put on some lip-gloss. Then, watch them using your mirror.

People can help

Use the people around you to cover your movements. Walk next to a family and blend with them. If someone is making a commotion, use the distraction to get closer to your suspect. Hide behind a grown-up to move across an open area.

Mix it up

Use your quick-change supplies to slip on a quick disguise. Or, take turns and let another Spygirl shadow the suspect for a while.

The quick change

Sometimes a spy must change how they look – and fast! Luckily, this is easy for girls. Just put a few extra things in your Spy Bag, and you'll be ready.

A hat or two

Hats are always a good idea. Try a baseball cap or a hat with a wide brim. Both can be pulled down low to hide your face.

Elastic hair bands

If you have long hair, you can use elastic hair bands to quickly change your hairstyle. Slip them into your pocket or tuck them into your Spy Kit.

Practice putting your hair up into a high ponytail and not pulling the last ends all the way through. This makes an easy bun. Stick on a baseball cap and your hair has disappeared!

Sunglasses

Every spy needs a good pair of dark sunglasses. People will have a hard time remembering your face if they can't see your eyes. Plus, no one will be able to see who or what you're looking at.

Jacket or sweater

Was that girl wearing blue or red? Confuse people by changing your clothes. Use colours that blend in, like white, grey, blue or black.

Start off with a sweater and then take it off to change your outfit. Or cover everything with a big jacket. Expert spies turn their coats inside out for a whole new look.

Even change your Spy Bag!

Tuck a large, re-usable shopping tote in your Spy Bag. Once you're done your quick change, put your Spy Bag inside your tote. Shopping anyone?

Body doubles

Here's a cool trick. If you think you are being tailed, try using a body double.

A body double looks like you and leads the enemy away while you do a quick change and escape.

Have another Spygirl dress exactly like you. Using a hat and sunglasses would be a good idea.

Your Spygirl friend waits at a planned meeting place where she can hide. It could be behind a store display or a large sign or in a store's changing room.

When you are being followed, take your time, but end up at the meeting place. As soon as you are hidden from view, stop.

Your Spygirl friend will step into view and keep on walking, pretending to be you.

You do a quick change and after a few minutes, go off in another direction.

Once you're safely away, the other Spygirl shows who she really is! She needs to act like she wasn't pretending to be you in the first place. Usually, taking off the hat will do the trick.

The enemy spy will see they've made a mistake, but won't know where you've gone!

Disguises

What if you want to want to observe a suspect, but can't shadow them because you're going to be stuck in one place, like a movie theatre? You don't want them to recognize you, but there's no place to hide.

In these cases, it's best to get in disguise. Dress differently than usual. Take on a new attitude. Change the way you move your body. Make sure you have the right props.

With a great disguise, the suspect will notice something unusual and may even look right at you. But they will be so distracted by your attitude, your clothes and your props, they won't even notice that it's you!

Here are some of my favourite disguises.

Girly girl

Clothes: Fancy dresses, skirts and tops with frills or sparkles. Shiny or furry jackets. A pretty purse. High-heeled shoes.

Hair and make-up: Styled hair. Curls, hair clips or hair bands. Pink lip-gloss. Dangly earrings.

Attitude: Stand tall with your chin up. Avoid mud-puddles and sports fields. Talk about fashion, famous singers or your dance classes.

Skater girl

Clothes: Jeans or long shorts. Trendy tee-shirt or tank top. Lots of layers under a baggy sweater or hoodie. Flat skater-style runners. If you can skate, bring along your board.

Hair and make-up: Short hair or loose long hair that is tousled, not styled. Try a cool hat, like a knitted beanie or a baseball cap with a skater brand name. No make-up.

Attitude: Slouch over when you walk. Lean against walls or railings. Don't be in a big hurry. Talk about skate tricks, biking or when you plan to go surfing.

Drama girl

Clothes: Long swishy skirts. Tops and jackets with fringes, ruffles or decorations. Crazy mix of styles and colours. Big, soft fabric purse. Flat black shoes or funky boots.

Hair and make-up: Big hair in wild styles. Use one-of-a-kind hair bands and clips. Bright sparkly eye shadow and lip-gloss. Dangly earrings. Lots of necklaces and bracelets.

Attitude: Don't be afraid to attract attention. Use lots of arm motions and plenty of emotion. Talk about serious actors, drama class or your last big audition.

Ninja girl

This disguise is used for times when you *don't* want to be seen.

Clothes: Tight fitting black pants and top. Quiet black shoes. Slim spy belt around your waist. Cover everything with a black jacket.

Hair and make-up: Smooth your hair back into a low ponytail. For shorter hair, part it on one side and sleek it down. No lipstick, but dark eyeliner would be cool.

Attitude: Quick, sly movements. Tuck into corners, behind lockers or inside doorways. Don't talk at all.

How to search a room

Your suspect is away and you need to find out what they're hiding, and fast!

Watch for traps

Before you go in the room or open anything, check for any traps. Watch for tape on the door frame or on drawers. Once the tape breaks, the suspect will know you've been there.

Smart searching

Take a good look around the room. Is there anything unusual or out of place?

Check the desk or dresser. Hunt for anything hidden on the bookshelves. Look inside small containers and drawers. Be sure to search underneath clothes or behind books. Don't forget to look under the bed and under the mattresses.

Anything hidden?

Be sure to check for secret hiding places. Is one shelf not as deep as the others? Is the storage box too shallow?

Does the closet seem extra narrow? Maybe there's a space hidden. Tap the wall or box to see if it sounds hollow and look for a tab to open it.

Spy tip: It's very important to make sure your search stays a secret. Put everything back exactly as you found it. And never read anyone's diary or journal. This is private!

Fingerprints

What if you think your suspect has been searching your room?

First, look to see whether anything has been disturbed. Then, check any disturbed spots for fingerprints.

Fingerprints are different for everybody. Match a mysterious fingerprint with a person, and you've got your suspect.

Finding and collecting a print

1. First look for sticky fingerprints on hard surfaces like glass, mirrors, desks or counters. If you find one, dust it lightly with baby powder.

2. If you can't see a print, try dusting where you *think* a print might be. Use your baby powder and brush.

3. Softly brush the prints with enough powder to show it clearly. Gently blow away any extra powder.

4. Press a piece of tape over the dusted print. Peel it away carefully.

5. Stick the tape on shiny black paper.

Shoe prints

If you are searching outside and the dirt is soft and damp, you could find a shoe print from your suspect.

Measure the shoe size using a measuring tape. Find out the shoe style. Did the shoe have high heels? Was it a flat flip-flop?

Check out the grip patterns on the bottom of runners to figure out the brand of shoe.

Draw or take a picture to help you remember.

Need to take a fingerprint?

1. Using the side of a lead pencil, rub a wide, dark mark on a piece of paper. Make sure it's big enough to fit a fingerprint.

2. Rub the finger on the black mark. Be sure it is covered with lead dust.

3. Press a piece of tape firmly onto the finger.

4. Gently peel off the tape.

5. Stick the tape to a white piece of paper.

6. Use a magnifying glass to compare the found print with the ones you've taken. Look for similar patterns.

Get-away plans

What if you're caught or someone spots you spying? This is no time for a chat. It's time to disappear.

Before you start a search, make an escape plan. Where is the nearest door? Is there another way out? Is there a place to hide if you can't get out?

When you are shadowing a suspect, keep an eye open for places to hide or disappear. This can be as easy as slipping into a shop in the mall or ducking behind a tree.

Spy tip: Plan ahead. Make up a good excuse to explain why you're there, just in case you're questioned.

Secret codes

Spygirls need to share the latest information on their suspects. Codes hide your messages from enemy spies. Important messages should always be sent in code.

The easiest codes are substitution codes, where one letter or number replaces another.

13-letter swap

Write down the first thirteen letters of the alphabet in a row. Underneath, match up the next thirteen letters. Use the matching letter in your message.

A B C D E F G H I J K L M

N O P Q R S T U V W X Y Z

MEET ME AT TWO
becomes
ZRRG ZR NG GJB

Key word swap

Use a key word to shift the alphabet over. Pick a word, like 'star', where no letter is used more than once.

Start your substitution with your key word. Then, use the rest of the alphabet. Skip over the letters you already used in your keyword.

Be sure to change the keyword often.

```
A B C D E F G H I J K L M N O P Q R S T U V W X Y Z
S T A R B C D E F G H I J K L M N O P Q U V W X Y Z
```

```
MEET ME AT TWO
```
becomes
```
JHHQ JH SQ QWL
```

Magazine code

Find a page in a magazine with lots of words. Use a pin to prick a tiny hole under the words you need for your message.

Pass the magazine to anther Spygirl. Tell her to read the interesting story about shoes.

To read the code, find the story and hold up that page to the light. Using a highlighter pen, mark each tiny hole you find.

Then, put the magazine down, find all the highlighter marks and write down the words to find the hidden message.

Breaking a code

Code breaking takes time. Use a pencil and have an eraser ready. Write out the coded message. Leave lots of space underneath it.

When you figure out one of the letters, write it every time you see that letter in your code.

Common words and patterns can help you break a code. Here are a few tips:

Single letters

There are only two letters that stand on their own. A and I. Look for these first.

Double letters

Not all letters like to hang out with their twin. Double vowels are EE or OO. Double consonants are DD, PP, LL, SS, MM and NN.

Common letters, common words

Try using the most common letters, E, H, S and T. Keep an eye out for the word THE, the most used three-letter word.

Vowels are needed

Each word must have at least one vowel. Check for patterns where A, E, I, O, U and even Y may fit.

Test your skills!

Here's a coded message to try to break.

Hint: you found this coded message when you were at the flower shop buying roses for your mother.

```
C   V C H H   I E E S   Y K T   F S   S V K
```

(see Page 37 for the answer key!)

Invisible ink

Writing in invisible ink can help keep your message a secret.

1. First, you need some soft wax from a white candle. Have a grown-up break off a piece of wax from a white candle that's been warmed up a bit.

2. Take the wax and roll it between your hands. Shape it into a crayon shape.

3. Take your new white wax crayon and write your message on white paper.

4. Write a decoy message in pen on top of your invisible message.

To see the invisible ink, take a pinch of cocoa powder and sprinkle it on the paper.

Using your finger, lightly rub the cocoa across the page.

The powder sticks to the wax and the message becomes visible!

Spy tip: Be smart. Even though your ink is invisible, make sure your message is in code.

Swaps and Drops

Now that your message is in code, how do you get it to another Spygirl without being seen? Try using a drop or a swap.

The message swap

Get two bags that look exactly the same. Keep one. The second bag goes to the other Spygirl. Arrange a time and place to do the swap.

Put the secret message in your bag. At the meeting place, put your bags down while you say hello. Then, pick up the other bag when you go. Your bag with the secret message goes with the other Spygirl. No one will know you made the swap.

Spy tip: This swap works if you need to swap spy stuff as well, like a hat for a disguise or a magnifying glass and fingerprint samples.

The dead drop

A dead drop is when you leave the item and walk away. Agree on a dead drop spot with another Spygirl. The spot needs to be easy to find, but not obvious to others.

Disguise your message and hide it in the dead drop spot.

Later on, the other Spygirl will go to the spot and pick up your message.

Cool dead drop spots

- Under the slide

- Behind a picture

- In a rock garden

- Inside a book in the library

- Under a chair or bench

Message disguises

- Wrap your message around a stick and cover with brown string.

- Tape your message on the back of a big leaf.

- Tape your message under a rock.

- Tuck your message inside a piece of newspaper.

- Leave your message inside a paper shopping bag

Spy tip: Be aware when using some drop locations, like in a mall. Your Spygirl friend better be there fast – otherwise mall security could find your message and throw it away!

Could you break the code?

Did you break the code on Page 31? Use a key word swap with **flower** as the key word.

F L O W E R A B C D G H I J K M N P Q S T U V X Y Z

A B C D E F G H I J K L M N O P Q R S T U V W X Y Z

Here is that message again:

C   V C H H   I E E S   Y K T   F S   S V K

SOLUTION: I will meet you at two

Signs and countersigns

If you can *see* another Spygirl but can't *talk* to her, you can still send a message.

Plan ahead for this and work out a secret code using body language.

Expert spies use everyday moves in a special combination to pass along messages.

Here are some ordinary moves:

- Tuck your hair behind your right ear

- Scratch your forehead

- Rub your nose

- Tie your left shoe

- Sneeze

- Cough

- Laugh

- Put on lip-gloss

- Read a magazine

- Pull on your ear or earring

- Twirl your necklace

- Check out your fingernails

Now, try these moves in a special order to send a message.

- Sneeze, rub your nose and pull on your earring means that the teacher is coming back to the classroom.

- Tie your shoe, check out your fingernails and tuck your hair behind your ear means that the suspect has left the playground.

- If you understand the message, let the other Spygirl know by twirling your necklace.

Other signs

Wear a special ring as a signal that you'll meet outside the music room after school.

Put your sweater on the back of your chair to let another Spygirl know there's a message waiting at the dead drop spot.

Spy supplies

A Spygirl needs to have her spy supplies ready at all times. For everyday spying, you only need a small Spy Kit. It can be hidden in your purse or backpack.

For bigger jobs, especially with disguises, you'll need a Spy Bag.

Spy Kit

A Spy Kit can be an empty mint tin or other small container with a lid that stays closed. You'll need to fit in:

- White wax invisible ink "crayon"

- White paper, cut or folded into small pieces

- Short wooden pencil

- Mini gel pen

- Elastics for your hair

Spy Bag

A Spy Bag needs to hold more supplies. Pick the best one for your mission and tuck in:

- Your smaller Spy Kit

- Quick-change supplies: hat, sweater, sunglasses

- Make-up mirror or compact

- Lip gloss

- Baby powder and a small make-up brush to check for fingerprints

- Cocoa powder to read invisible ink

- Wide clear tape (not magic tape)

- Shiny black paper

- Magnifying glass

- Measuring tape

- Flashlight

- Thin cotton gloves, white or black

- String, scissors and large paper clips, to fish things out of a tight spot or from behind someone's back

- Water and snacks, when you will be out on a long mission (bring quiet snacks - not chips in noisy packages!)

- Plastic snack bags that can zip closed, for storing evidence

- Camera (or camera phone)

- Watch (or clock on your phone)

Spy tip: Powders can be tricky to carry and messy to use. Measure out a tablespoon of each powder and store it in a small container with a secure lid. Round, plastic pill containers work well and snap closed.

Final tips

Congratulations! You now have the skills you need to start spying!

Design your own disguises. Make your own secret codes. Share these spy skills with your best friends.

And remember, if you ever discover something that makes you uncomfortable or nervous, be sure to tell a grown-up.

Have fun and stay safe!

Want more?

Visit www.spyskillsforgirls.com
for photos, videos and more!

CPSIA information can be obtained
at www.ICGtesting.com
Printed in the USA
LVOW01s0855271215
467669LV00094B/2722/P

9 780987 876621